T0335336

ADMISSION

ADMISSION

POEMS BY

JERRY WILLIAMS

CARNEGIE MELLON UNIVERSITY PRESS
PITTSBURGH 2010

ACKNOWLEDGMENTS

The following journals were kind enough to publish selections from this book:
Barrow Street, Brooklyn Review, Drunken Boat, Evergreen Review, Icon, Margie, Minnesota Review, New Ohio Review, Pleiades, Texas Review, Tin House, and *Witness.*

The author is grateful for permission to include excerpts from the following previously copyrighted material:

"Ashes of American Flags" by Jeff Tweedy and Jay Bennett. ©2002 by Warner-Tamerlane Publishing Corporation, Words Ampersand Music (administered by Warner-Tamerlane Publishing Corporation), and You Want a Piece of This Music (administered by Bug Music). All rights reserved. Used by permission of Alfred Publishing Company and Bug Music.

Zen Mind, Beginner's Mind by Shunryu Suzuki; protected under the terms of the International Copyright Union ©2006. Reprinted by arrangement with Shambhala Publications, www.shambhala.com.

Many thanks to Connie Amoroso, Ravindra Bagal and family (belatedly), Tony Chaney, Mark Conard, Gerald Costanzo, Peter Covino, Tom Dvorske, Timothy Fox, Aaron Gwyn, Margaret Kearns-Stanley, Cynthia Lamb, Ronald Mancini, Marymount Manhattan College, Kate Mele, Monica Richart, Edward Walkiewicz, and Greg Williams.

The publication of this book is supported by a grant from the Pennsylvania Council on the Arts.

PENNSYLVANIA
COUNCIL
ON THE
ARTS

Library of Congress Control Number 2009930167
ISBN 978-0-88748-522-0

10   9   8   7   6   5   4   3   2   1

for Shelby

CONTENTS

III. Red

I would like to salute
the ashes of American flags

—Wilco, from "Ashes of American Flags"

I. GRAY

UNADORNED

I let a dog in the park lick my face for you.
I pretended not to know the murder rate in Denmark for you.
I've tried to stay ugly for you.
I turned myself into an oil field, switched on the klieg lights
      for you, and let Texaco start drilling.
I never thought about the future for you or else I thought about it
      in terms that only you could understand,
        though we had never actually met.
I worked in a cardboard box factory for you.
I gave up skin for you.
Whenever love metastasized, I ran over it with my lawnmower
      for you.
I wrote "Stairway to Heaven" for you.
I did the whole Reverend Dimmesdale thing for you.
For you, I tramped around town smelling old books and thinking
      of better days.
If it weren't for you, I might have thrown open the door to any
      number of empty apartments and gone straight
        for the knife drawer.
I quit the team for you, I quit the band for you.
I survived—for you—a *major* stork attack at the free clinic.
I romanticized the Russian Revolution for you.
All that weight and all those miles for you.
For ages, I drove really shitty cars for you, cars with bald tires, cars
      that burned a quart of Quaker State a day,
        cars with no reverse.
I passed the Clean Hair Act of 1992 for you.
I took the pill for you.
I took my pulse pass/fail for you.

I took all the wheelchairs out of this poem for you.

I scrutinized the maps of various principalities and prowled around
　　the depths of their free print media,
　　　　scavenging underground for you.

I've stood at the podium and knelt at the peephole for you.

One night I camped out on the sidewalk to protest against
　　something for you—I can't remember what it was—
　　but I'm sure nothing was ever done.

I had my juvenile criminal record expunged for you.

I secretly hoarded food for you.

For you, I've spent fifteen of the last twenty-two Christmases alone
　　on the couch with *The Catcher in the Rye*.

For you, I've suffered bouts of Pernicious Cubical Zombification
　　that no amount of Prison Movie Therapy could cure.

I fell this far without you for you.

Anyone goodhearted or wounded enough to fill in for you got
　　bombarded with encrypted code left over
　　　　from the War of Adolescence which, by the way—
　　totally based on false intelligence.

For you to believe a word I'm saying, you have to admit that when　．
　　my hand floated palely away, I forgot
　　every single breast I've ever touched.

This is me trying to settle down for you.

This is me putting my bullhorn and my guillotine
　　in the attic for you.

I'm turning gray for you.

So, please, tell me

when will you be born?

BEHOLD THE FATHER

When I was eleven years old
my father tried to convince me
that the word *nigger* is in the dictionary.
He claimed the epithet does not derive
from any linguistic ill will
on the part of white people:
They simply applied an existing term
to a developing anthropology.
"It means bad person," he insisted,
his right hand slicing the air.
And we could have looked it up, too,
if we'd had a dictionary in the house,
but we didn't live in that kind of a house.
Either you took the boss's word for it
or you kept your doubts to yourself.

Last December my father got the hook.
He died in his sleep of something akin to loneliness.
I hadn't spoken to him in seventeen years,
and I almost forget why.
I didn't make it to the funeral,
I didn't scrutinize the photographs
of him in his temporary casket,
I didn't even meet my sisters and my mother
in Kentucky when they scattered
his ashes on Pine Mountain,
ashes they'd had to purchase from his widow.
I suppose I wanted to hold on
to my resentment for a few more years.

Or else I was too embarrassed to let it go
after having nourished it for so long
with gimlets and address changes
and not enough shoreline or keystrokes or dawns.
At times, I think it would have been better
for all of us if he'd never lived,
and then some totally unexpected hearsay
will bubble up from the depths,
undeniably molten and true,
as when a fellow by the name of Fletcher
tracked down one of my sisters
to pay his respects and testify to what
a decent and generous man my father was.
Back in the seventies, Fletcher had
worked his way up from hod carrier
to bricklayer to foreman
in my father's construction company.
He had a good life, a nice home.
Four of his five children went to college.
"I owe it all to Dave," Fletcher said.
"In those days nobody would give
a black man that much responsibility."

Here's where I say: *It doesn't make sense.*
Here's where I say: *What happened*
to the gun-toting, adulterous welsher
who only ever did anything for anyone
so he could feel like a big shot?
Here's where I say: *Behold!*
the insipid villainy of the father.
But I can't seem to whip myself

into the appropriate frenzy.
What would be the point?
Dying is like paying off your debts
with money you found in the trash.

No expectations, no grudges, no noise—
just the low-toned gurgle of the living
as they conduct their underwater interrogations
in a language all covered with scars.

I Think I Know Her Name

When I don't drink
my subconscious, my so-called past,
the lie experience told my dreams,
attacks me in my sleep
and when I wake up
with my face all distorted,
some love not quite turning out
the way I thought it would,
I put on my robe,
pump the coffeemaker for information,
check my messages.

Enough said.

That *was* going to be
the first—what?—line,
and now you're thinking it,
dear rubbernecker,
so it might as well be groaned.
This is what happens
when you realize your world
isn't just climbing on top
of some form of public transportation
and grabbing the nearest wire,
the nearest cable,
the copper passage,
the twisted cord,
the soldered connection,
electrified and so much better than you are

and not very nice
or otherwise testimonial.
You should quit while you're ahead,
and you know it.

So now for the grit:
The bartender's hips in gray slacks—
her face is too heartbreaking to mention—
remind me that I am human
and seriously ready
to stop eavesdropping
on other people's conversations
to accumulate
my quota of civilization points.
I am still a man,
despite what necessity demands,
despite what Exley called
the journey on a davenport.
Above the stench of this beer hall
and the worthlessness
of my American concerns,
something smells   very, very good.

GALLERY DAY WITH SEAN

Here's how it worked:
Sean would burst
into the gallery and
snap off a judgment.

This is interesting,
and we browsed.
*This is a waste
of time,* and we fled.

His process reminded
me of my editing days.
You had to skin the
envelope, scoop out

the insides, study
the contour of the font,
taste a few lines.
The least imperfection

and you hauled off
and fired that poet's
submission right
back to the kitchen,

like an entrée
with a hair in it
or a side dish
with a hair in it.

Chelsea's pre-museum
song goes on forever,
but an afternoon
consists of a limited

array of notes.
Must not tarry.
Must not wipe your
feet on the synthetic

intestine doormat.
Or frown at an oak
tree cordoned off
with razor wire,

total mystification
followed by demystification.
The smell of crayons
and the stylishness

of George Washington's
bob on the dollar bill
no longer essential scenarios.
The new human being

wears a dirty ski mask;
he plays endless games
of pocket pool; he waits
for Jesus to hand

over the lottery numbers.
Sean reacted to this
Robinson Crusoe art
like I once reacted to

pretentious line breaks,
indebted metaphors,
and weird grammatical tics.
Images floating in the

crevasses of influence,
zero faith in literality.
New York has run out
of good refuse, Sean

announced at some point.
Collagists drive all the way
to Chicago to find the junk
they need, stay in a hotel,

wander the streets
with a shopping cart.
Sean was a pro,
but some of what I saw

that day seemed fresh
and fun—there, I said it.
Inexperience rejuvenated
me to the core.

A willingness to
acknowledge that turtles
do, in fact, make a ton
of noise undisrupted me.

Back before I lost my
innocence, a poem could
stand in the middle
of the Brooklyn Bridge

and pulsate with the
grief of a dying moon.
I filtered nothing.
I assumed nothing.

Though the bridge was
a field in Ohio and I
pushed my hair out of my
eyes and said, "Whoa!"

Flying United

Whenever I'm feeling low I like to hop a flight to Vegas
on the airline whose aptly gray planes are the easiest
to hijack and dive-bomb into the World Trade Center
     and the Pentagon.
I'm not talking about the T-word; I'm talking about taking
advantage of a situation; I'm talking about economy.
And I don't care whether or not James Dickey actually came up
with "fly the friendly skies" when he worked as an ad man
     in Chicago.
This silly factoid has been stuck to my recollection for so long
the halituous ramblings of a thousand false martyrs couldn't
     burn it off.
Poor James Dickey, so unfortunately named and a posthumous liar
     to boot.
The skies are anything but friendly.
For instance:
My sister's a mechanic for the aforementioned bombardier
and now will never see the retroactive cost of living raise
the company promised her union ten years ago.
"Labor *Jihad* !" I advised her in an e-mail transmission—
just before AOL Time Warner Nabisco Pfizer cut off
     my internet access.
So I'm sitting on this 757, knocking back a Xanax,
and an Arab couple slips down the aisle with their teenage son.
All three are wearing New York Yankees caps
and they have this look in their eyes like every single
white person on the plane has explosives strapped to their chest.
I want to help these people
stow their suitcases in the overhead compartment.

I want to gather their dark portrayals unto my bosom.
But I feel an amateur historian's fugue coming on:
Osama bin Carter, Osama bin Reagan, Osama bin Bush,
Osama bin Clinton, Osama bin Junior, Osama bin Spielberg,
Osama bin Rumsfeld, Osama bin Albright, Osama bin Zeta-Jones,
Osama Cat Stevens, Osama bin Kissinger, Osama bin Hitchens.
By the time the plane reaches altitude, I've implicated everyone
from Euclid to the Dallas Cowboy cheerleaders.
It's too simple to simply blame the enemy.
Culpability is an airborne bio-toxin that nation-states inhale
            through the eyes;
it smells like fuel oil and forward motion.
Consider the case of young Bob McIlvaine, twenty-six years old,
perished, extinguished, murdered, unplugged,
wasted, abolished, man-slaughtered, collaterally damaged.
And for what? Nine hundred years of history?
Nobody deserves that.
He stumbled out of the South Tower and crossed Liberty Street,
only to be put out of his happiness by falling debris,
his penultimate thought *I made it* and not *Fuck, that's hot*
or
I wonder if I'll black out before I hit the ground.
At least his loving parents can keep that in mind when they're
funding scholarships and weeping phosphorescently
            in front of Congress.
Not so suddenly, the seatbelt light goes pong
and the aircraft banks into a turn, begins its descent.
Every head in the cabin chants, *What-if-what-if-what-if*?
I slide my plastic window shade up and a spritz
of desert light lands on the empty seat beside me.
This might be completely irrelevant, but I was in love once.

She was fifteen and I was sixteen.

For elocutionary purposes, I'll call her the Scar. *E pluribus unum.*

I think she peed her pants the first time we made out

in the back of the bus coming home from the Roth game.

A wet spot appeared.

Her Italian-American father, literally, worked in a chocolate factory.

He gargled eight ounces of salt water every morning

and brutalized his children with belts, deprivation, and the palm
       of his hand.

I wanted to be the *man*, to figure out a way to protect my little
       ruination,

so I reported the coward to Social Services.

A heavyset woman with no briefcase showed up at their house

and spoke to the family in the living room, surrounded by
       cream-colored doilies

and crucifixes and pictures of saints with rosaries draped
       around the frames.

The minute she walked out the door,

Scar said her father slapped her younger brother across the face.

Now I'm wondering what might have happened that could have
       changed things—

negotiation, apology, more firepower, books, cheese,
       non-involvement.

Remember this if nothing else: My life is based on a true story.

When that landing gear oozes into place and the captain
       starts his approach

and I look out my window at a three-quarter-sized Eiffel Tower

straddling a parking garage and across the boulevard a giant black

pyramid trolls for gambling addicts in outer space,

I realize, with the voltage of a Taser jab,

that no one in Iraq or Afghanistan or the former Yugoslavia

will ever be privileged enough to go as far into debt as I am. In an hour, I'll be hunched over a five-dollar table at Binion's, content to be baffled and alive and patriotically blowing money, safer in Las Vegas than in a womb.

Imaginary Family Vacation

Dad's out front in his rocking chair finishing
The New York Times crossword puzzle from last Wednesday.
Still wearing her running shorts,
Mom's in the kitchen perfecting a risotto recipe.
My sister Julianne is down by the lake hunting
for the ideal specimen of zebra swallowtail butterfly.
She's an entomology major, which I find disgusting.
Sitting on the porch, I say to my dad,
"We read *The Jungle* last week in English,"
and he says, "You know, Upton Sinclair ran
for the House in 1920 and the Senate in 1922
as a Socialist—state of California."
"Cool," I say, looking around for an arrowhead.
Julianne walks across the gravel road,
cupping something in her hands, all serious looking.
As she reaches the porch, my mother
comes outside with a spoonful of risotto for me to taste.
The leaves are on the verge of exploding with color.
A light breeze suggests the dankness of lake water.

Then, with the sound of breaking bones,
a rusty Chevy Nova with Ohio plates stops along the road.
An older couple disembarks: They're alternating driving duties.
The car hiccups and hiccups and stalls.
Someone in the backseat snickers and the father grabs
the kid by the shirt and pulls him forward, hard,
calls him a wild animal,
and shoves him back into place.
He climbs in the car and jerks the passenger door shut.

Dad glances over at me, and Julianne says, "Jesus Christ."
Mom returns to the kitchen in silence.
I feel like I'm watching creatures from another planet
trying to get their spaceship started.
Nevertheless, some familiar magnetism brings me to my feet
and I move unconsciously toward the Nova.
A grave mistake has been made.
"Where are you going?" my dad says, but I'm already gone.
I'm already knocking on the passenger's side window,
the man is already opening the door,
I'm already sliding into the backseat where I belong.

The Meanest Buddhist I Ever Met

Close-cropped hair. Check.

Daily meditation. Check.

Truncated pastorals up the wazoo. Check.

Wife named after foliage. Check.

Founded his own poetry publisher in the kitchen
with an old printing press. Check.

Personal essays about being assaulted
in reform school. Check.

Anti-war activist. Check.

Says he wouldn't hurt a fly. Check.

Red in the face. Check.

Big fat vein pulsating in the middle
of his forehead. Check.

EXPECTANCY

I sometimes happen
upon your kind
browsing through the produce section
or waiting in line at the post office,
your skin so pale,
your stride surprisingly athletic,
an inextinguishable skit of womanliness
in all your parts.
But it's not the breasts
or the hips
or the protuberance
that burn,
it's the *rhetoric* of your looming—
suburban and reckless,
lurid and luminescent.
At such times,
I am so overcome with longing
that I look away.
Poets have no access
to the gene pool.
Now here you are,
someone I once lucked into loving,
hoisting creation up
a flight of steps,
five months gone
with another man's work.
This could be
the only chance I ever get
to be my own redeemer

so please
do me this kindness
before a continent of bad timing
clears its throat
and turns to news.
Give me your
shallow, draining breath
that smells of vitamins and citrus.
Give me your lips
free of wine
yet moist with possibility.
Give me your tongue
when it's slow and heavy
like an hour
of island sleep.
Give me your commissure
and your apex
and your median lingual sulcus.
Give me your saliva
as a palliative,
and let me pretend
you recline in our own bath
with that white watermelon
rising out of sudsy water,
all pristine and friendly.
In case the apologetic truth
takes my entire life hostage,
let me pretend.

II. Black

Jimmy Huber's Jeremiad

When the change machine at the laundromat runs out of quarters—
that's terrorism.

If an SUV won't let you merge into traffic on Interstate 95,
the driver must be late for a car-bomb attack on a market
or shopping district.

Canker sores on the tongue, gin blossoms, persistent
hematospermia: These are all cowardly acts of genetic terrorism.

Iraqi and Afghani civilians splashing brain matter
on a Navy SEAL's new uniform.
You better believe that's terrorism.

All next-door neighbors are state-sponsored terrorists.

My balls itch! Terrorism!

That random fettuccini alfredo smell in the locker room
at the gym. Now that's domestic terrorism.

Dentists are terrorists. *Highlights Magazine* was a front.

Crushed ice, v-neck T-shirts, and parking garages
were invented by terrorists.

The ocean is no different from a Ryder truck stuffed with C-4
and set for remote detonation.

The fact that they won't give you nitrous oxide
when you get a haircut. Terrorism.

Bing Crosby was a terrorist and so was Burl Ives, and Rudolph
smuggled depleted uranium in his nose.

Stand-up comedians and male cheerleaders are limited
political terrorists.
May they be stricken with Guantanamo Insomnia.

Anyone who owns a ukulele or a magnet is automatically
a terrorist.

The sound of chalk on the sidewalk is a terrorist.

Snow is a terrorist.

Overconfident bureaucrats with watermelon-sized heads
who never let people finish their sentences
trend toward skyjacking and hostage-taking.

Unborn fetuses fund terrorism.

Every Bob Seger song you hear on the radio puts another
fragmentary grenade into the sweaty hands
of an international terrorist. Ditto the Beatles and Queen.

Recycling is obviously terrorism.

Those fake trolley cars with real tires and low self-esteem might
as well be transporting a bunch of nature poets (i.e., terrorists)

to a homicide bombing at a disco.

The moon is a revolutionary terrorist.

The stars are zits on a suicide bomber's back.

Darwinism is cause-based terrorism.

When a bomb goes off in a café or restaurant, blame the onions.

Everything anyone says and everything anyone does
is made of weapons-grade material.

Both the noumenal and the phenomenal are terrorists:
The leaves on the trees are code green, the sky is code blue,
the dandelions are code yellow, the cat is code orange,
and the barn is code red.

We're all dead.

IMPRINTING

Whenever anyone asked the father
what was playing at the movies
or what was on television
or who was making all that noise in the attic,
his answer would always be the same:
Deaf and dumb woman showing a blind man her ass.
Then he'd lean back in his chair,
ransack his two-day growth of beard,
and snort contentedly.
If you wanted your answer,
you had to investigate on your own.
But first you had to gain control
of the necessary mode of inquiry—
Dayton Daily News, TV Guide, Black & Decker flashlight.
This was no easy task.
The father was cagey and quick.
Snatching the item from his grasp took ten or fifteen tries.
Deaf and dumb woman showing a blind man her ass.
He spoke with an exaggerated southern drawl,
pronouncing *deaf* as if it were spelled *D-E-E-F,*
clearly blaming the cracker within himself.
And, of course, they all laughed, the whole family,
this being the longest running joke of the decade.

Years later, the son would wonder how much
that portrait of unattainability
had influenced his outlook on the world.
He wondered if being party to the father's constant
sarcasm had turned him

into a half-empty rather than a half-full type of individual.
Or if he'd simply been infused
with a heightened sense of irony.
The answer lies in the image itself.
A voluptuous woman with long black hair
presents her perfect round ass to a man who has no eyes
to see it with and seems to have no hands to touch it with,
no idea he's in the presence of such beauty.
There's only a small distance between them,
but she's deaf. She could not hear the man
if he cried out, "I am blind! What is happening to me?"
and she couldn't reply even if she did hear him,
for she has no voice.
The son can envision their disconcerted faces,
their straining gestures.
They are lewd yet toilsome,
weary as medicated glaciers.
They are the saddest people on earth.

Menstruation Blues

As a girl of a certain age—
fifteen, tops—
this could not have been her first mystery play.

Lying on my mother's bed.

No one home.
No one home as usual.

Her eyes said cramps.

Her eyes said I don't think I can stand the shedding
of my insides a minimum of 425 times
over the course of my life.

Her eyes said you worthless piece of shit.

A girl of a certain age,
she looked like a tomato about to explode,
fully clothed,
describing an abstract pain
I did not have the clearance to understand.

I imagined ceremonial evisceration
at the hands of her Roman forebears:
First you get the knives, the skewers,
the red hot pincers and then—
you get the pear of anguish.

A girl of a certain age.

I would have climbed inside
the iron maiden of her grimace,
multiplied dirt bike accident
by crashing through sliding-glass door
but nothing I cooed,
nothing I touched with my knuckle-hands,
nothing I offered to obtain
could appease her.

A boy of a certain age—
sixteen, tops—
I dialed zero and asked for 911,
partly out of spite,
partly out of hedging concern
that she might not be overreacting,
that my knowledge of her plumbing
was a vacant lot next to a clipboard factory.

Tranquility issued from the promise
of community intervention.

All hail the gestalt of blood!

Three powerful raps at the door
meant two men (and a gurney)
with pickup and delivery on their minds.

A girl of a certain age
never folds under questioning.
She sticks to her bible story.

Are you family? asked the man
whose breath smelled like hospital.

No? he said.

Then follow us, if you like,
in the car you don't have.

FROM A TRAVEL BRIEF

Therefore, it might be
something simple:
a woman in a Bronx subway car
reading a Polish newspaper
and another, younger woman
who sits down beside her
and opens a Polish novel.
They notice each other.
They laugh out loud,
say hello and yesyes
in their native tongue,
then they return to their
respective quietude,
surprised and yet not surprised.
These two women found
each other in a language
they had been asked to forget.
Miles from home,
their separate eras confiding.
Whatever they thought familiar
refracted in the mind.
And still they seem okay—
more than okay.

Love and Oncology

When my mother got cancer
I thought of an old Polaroid I'd found
in her dresser drawer when I was twelve.
She was standing in front of a white wall
in her bra and panties (like a hostage).
When my mother got cancer
I hoped she might lose some weight
but she's the Belle of Appalachia.
When my mother got cancer
I sat on my bathroom floor
in bitchy Rhode Island and diffracted.
I guilted a neighbor into feeding my fish
and caught a flight to Tennessee.
When my mother got cancer
I put my hand on her back
and whispered something tribal in her ear.
When my mother got cancer
I blamed coal, I blamed straight pipes
pumping human waste into rivers—
because if I didn't I would always hear that ticking.
When my mother got cancer
the nomenclature was excruciating:
incision, J-pouch, temporary colostomy,
napalm, Agent Orange.
When my mother got cancer
there was no more mention of treadmills
or trips out west or too many pain pills.
When my mother got cancer
I let a doctor stick his finger up my ass

44

and gamely set a date for the fiber-optic snake.
When my mother got cancer
I tried to put it out of my mind.
I went to bars and got drunk and started
arguments with the unemployed about unions.
When my mother got cancer
I swear it was true love.
The world fit perfectly into a powdered latex glove.

A New Doctrine

Cruise missiles should never miss
the target, baby, but sometimes they do.

There's milk to be had
if the cow can be secured.

When you bump your head on the corner
of a kitchen cabinet, think of sand.

Love of country smells like barbecued paranoia
when it's ripping you to shreds.

Apply bumper stickers and ribbons
to all wounds.

Stand in the middle of 51st Street with no alternative
and hate yourself until the cops come.

Attribute all defiance to a misinterpretation
of Jefferson, Jesus, and J.D. Salinger.

Now put your wrists together.
Now swallow.

Harry and Bess

Harry opens the car door and falls into the front yard.
Moonlight turns the rain to burnished wire.
Thinking a natural emetic might remind the evening
to play chamber music instead of opera,
he takes a deep, guttural breath—and lets go.
Way past empty, way past reflection,
he stands on his knees, all but drenched,
tips his head back and swallows a mouthful
of rainwater that tastes like a silver dollar smells.
He slams the car door to stop the murderous chiming.
Does it matter that he's late coming to ground
or that he's hammered drunk? Does it matter
that driving home from the bar nearly made him
a sitting duck for the flimflam of local tragedy?
Bess thinks it matters, and she's inside
their mostly yellow house loading a new battery
into the smoke alarm, always the watchful assistant.
How will she react to the purple impressions
of fingers and knuckles now blooming
like dirty orchids across his middle,
the grim result of an even grimmer proposition
that his puzzled colleagues buy him drinks
in exchange for punching him in the stomach?
Harry can see frenetically choreographed phone calls
to in-laws and lawyers in his future—
dark, annulling blood in the drains.
Bess has spent too much time with the sofa
and the lamps to fall for such incompetent misdirection.
Enough is enough *is* enough. Harry and Bess

might as well be magicians for all their years
of repetition and consultation and fading,
their shared history of innocent gestures covering up
momentous verdicts, their proud tolerance for pain.
Why else would they know that the greatest feats
of legerdemain depend on the simplest falsehoods
and that anything in this world can suddenly   disappear?

Gem City

City that popped me out of a slice of exodus
then promptly unmothered me.
City of fixed whiffleball games.
City of brick poltergeists and nauseous trees.
City where the suicide hotline lady calls *you*.
City that protects fervently the rights of the mediocre.
Former union-friendly city.
City of paltry public transit.
City that cut into me like a stripe.
City of failed accords.
City with too many cops and not enough robbers.
City of none of my great loves.
Unbelievably segregated city.
City that holds grown men hostage in their mothers's basements,
clutching their guts in agony with nerve-damaged hands.
City that lied about inventing aviation.
City that gives you a little cup of pills every morning.
City of weird smells and walking coffins.
City where musicians play Wagner with suction cups.
City of bologna and diet cola.
City of eternal optometry.
Empty cash register city.
City that discarded its *volta*.
City that worships floods and tornados.
City of escape artists and name changers.
City that inhales apology and exhales blame.

POEM FOR MY GODSON

Owen Mack Carlson, born May 7, 2004

I could hear you howling in the background
when your father called me from the hospital
the day after you were born,
surly and perhaps a bit too lean.
"The OR looked like a crime scene," he said.
"They finally had to put a plastic tarp down."
For twenty-eight hours your mother labored
to expel you, glazed with fire, into her arms,
your head somewhat misshapen from the havoc.
Outside, the traffic mutely sluiced
down Wilshire Boulevard
and for once it didn't count.
Sanction and retribution and post-industrial panic,
the Apocalypse as foreign policy,
the refusal of the bomb to pay a living wage to the sky—
all the horrible errata in this world no longer horrify
because you're here, you're out, you're free.
No doubt you'll be handsome like your parents,
keen of heart and mind like your parents,
idealistic like your parents.
When you're older maybe you'll agitate for change,
maybe you'll find the answers on the field
or in the flesh or in a manifesto of fractals,
maybe you'll build something beautiful with your hands
and give it away. So don't be shy.
Wade out into your life and find your tribe.
Stay informed, write things down,

learn to play an instrument.
Take heed of people who can tell you about failure.
Risk everything, gamble nothing,
and worship no god but love.
Know that even if you get lost
you will never be alone.

PAINKILLER NIGHTMARE

I walk into the free clinic, ask for a complete workup,
and this obscenely beautiful nurse hands me
an inch-thick packet of forms and a pencil.
The physician, played by Alec Baldwin,
uncharacteristically presides over the dingiest of waiting rooms.
I say *uncharacteristically* because aren't doctors
always in their offices putting golf balls
into bedpans and lying to their wives on speakerphone?
In the dream I shout, "Hey, I have a friend who wrote
an article for *Penthouse* about seeing a hypnotist
for non-surgical penis enlargement therapy,"
and Baldwin starts in with the side-splitting laughter.
He falls to the floor and rolls over on his back,
howling at the dirty ceiling like a blooper.
Suddenly, it dawns on me that a complete workup
involves the dreaded Q-tip test and before I can escape
a naked homunculus with a massive scabby penis
scurries out of the inner office pursued
by two burly, *Cuckoo's Nest* type orderlies.
They corner the little guy, sedate him, and drag him away.
Now I'm spooked. I head for the door and one of the orderlies
grabs me and pushes me toward an antique weight scale.
When I resist he wrestles me to the ground,
applying his signature *pro forma* leg lock.
We're sitting there perfectly, inexorably still,
even as the far wall melts and a step aerobics class appears.
I commence begging in a soft, sarcastic voice: "Help me. Help me."
But nary an aerobicizer reacts. I'm scared out of my mind,
although the orderly assures me that *everything's gonna be fine*

if I'll juuust relaaaaax . . .
and right when I'm about to surprise him
with a major karate chop to the neck,
right when I organize my hand into practically an axe blade—
well, you know what happens.

III. Red

Admission

"If an artist becomes too idealistic, he will commit suicide, because between his ideal and his actual ability there is a great gap. Because there is no bridge long enough to go across the gap, he will begin to despair. That is the usual spiritual way."

—Shunryu Suzuki, from *Zen Mind, Beginner's Mind*

An autumn shadow draws across my room.
This morning's remedy hasn't yet kicked in.
I'm losing the bookshelf wars.
Not to a doctor, but to a dream horizon
dotted with enormous nylon sacks
of arrogance and longing and gloom-fueled sloth.
I wanted more. There it is.
I wanted so much more to issue forth.
Wrong or right, I wanted to walk under a bridge
wearing a hat made of prose
and sing Buddy Holly songs in Russian.
I wanted to sell fire and sirens door to door.
Forget the stamen and the pistil.
I wanted a soy toy. I wanted more.
I could eat the breeze right off the curtains.
I wanted to get to the point where what I'm allowed
actually feels like what I desire.
Maybe I should have married A, B, C, D, E, F, G,
and all the rest, but I had to child-proof my entire future,
stand on the roof with a shotgun diploma,
and campaign for National Verb Month.
I wanted to arrive at a different concourse.
I wanted the perfect outlet

for whatever coal dust I might cough up.

I wanted exploits, vehemence, divergence,

characters screaming at each other on stage,

slicing off fingers and chucking them

into the prop sink and then laughing their guts out,

doubled over, tears streaming down their faces,

guffawing, blood up and down their forearms,

gravel and pulverized antiquities underfoot.

No big deal. No human pyramids.

I wanted to love someone so hard

she would never forgive me.

I wanted to rob a bank with a golf club.

I expected more from myself.

I wish I heard voices.

I wish piñatas were filled with naked students and Vicodin.

I thought I would be the scariest mummy

in the museum by now,

but all I am is preparedness,

the implements of my sterility laid out in the dusk.

This here: This is not even what I wanted to say.

I've failed at reverse prayer,

failed to really understand my own eyes.

It's getting dark and I can hear my neighbors creaking.

They must hide the pigeons at night.

My greatest fear is that the love of my life

will be the one who pushes the needle,

the one who tells me to start counting backwards

from forever.

THE GUY WHO READ BEFORE BOB

Often the voice did not
match the amateur lumberjack.

I listened to every word
except the ones that sounded

like witches burned at the stake,
an amazingly formal atrocity.

The man cheated life: He loved
the story of his dead girlfriend,

ears with a corpse attached,
but he refused to look at

his own bruises and wormholes.
Big Apple Dumpling Gang

That Couldn't Shoot Straight.
The more impenetrable the poem

the more between-poem rap
as if clarification were the show

and the poem the commercial.
So many expressions,

so many impersonal tongues,
every additional syllable another

rock piled upon the accused.
Thus, the poet's attempt

to convince the audience
they weren't sitting in purgatory

failed.

HBO

Would you fellate the headsman to guarantee a sharper,
more oblique-edged guillotine blade.

If you had to choose between eating a man's feces and killing him,
would you choose murder.

Would gender make a difference.

If Siamese twins masturbate, is that incest.

How long should the average suicide note be.

Would you sooner bleed to death or freeze to death.

Have you ever stood up too fast and felt yourself closing in
on Hallelujahville.

Do you see why it hurts to be human. Why it hurts to be
one or the other.

Would you rather lie in bed at night with your eyes open or sit
down to a one-man meal hosted by refrigerator hum.

THE TONIGHT SHOW

After every single game
and most practices
we sat in the family room
with the television off.
My father apostrophized
while I stared at a row
of wooden geese with artificial
gold-plated wings flying
across the manila wall,
suffering through a ruthless,
two-hour critique of my shooting,
my defense, my passing and rebounding—
even my timeout huddle posture.
You didn't need to be Greek
to recognize the unwholesomeness
of this father-son fiasco.
Hence, the geese and the staring
and the migraines that arrived,
like wages, twice a month.
Sick headaches, my mother
called them in the original Hillbilly.
The pain started in my eyes,
luminosity burned, and the borders
of objects and faces wavered.
Inside of an hour, I lay flat
on my back with the lights out,
quietly moaning to myself
as sulfuric acid sloshed around
the mutiny of my cortex.

My mother would bring me
a warm dishrag for my forehead
and a worthless pill to dissolve
under my tongue. The hours passed
in gong-like fashion and just before
Ed McMahon introduced Johnny Carson
I would vomit in the trashcan
my mother left by the side of the bed,
and the pain simply
resolved itself and floated away.
I will never forget the sweet relief
of walking down the gangplank
to where my parents sat
waiting for *The Tonight Show*
and drinking sulfuric acid
by the glassful. They let me sit in front
of the television and watch Carson
whose squinting, paternal laughter
signaled the end of an ordeal.
Life seemed to begin anew
right there in the family room
with Burbank gleaming like Ithaca
in a completely different time zone.

Exegesis of a Hard Case

I have endured four major breakups in my life. Each one nearly killed me. Without a two-month grief regimen of unintentional dieting, weightlifting, sofa catatonia, and benzodiazepines, I might never have survived. What's more, a number of lesser disintegrations have compromised my brittle nervous system. I have been the dumper as well as the dumpee, and neither role obtains. I have cheated and been cheated on. (Once, I pulled a reverse cuckold.) I have relocated, disappeared, or simply faded away, and I have found myself on the receiving end of this same sad protocol. I have split up in person, over the telephone, via e-mail and the United States Postal Service—even on cassette tape. The means did not always justify the ends; the reasoning was not always sound. I have retracted pronouncements, negotiated for more time, and confessed all my sins in a convulsion of jealousy. I have wept uncontrollably and inspired uncontrollable weeping. I have begged for mercy and demanded apology and been denied both. I have pleaded and fallen silent. I have ignored or been ignored. I have wrapped myself in a red flag for comfort. I have heard the words *I can't do this anymore* and *I don't want you to go*, and I have spoken them myself. I have packed up all my belongings or helped someone else pack. I have driven away in trucks and vans, checked into motels, and slept on friends' couches. I have assessed blame and remembered fondly and felt unable to let go. Telephone calls for years. I have borne grudges and, no doubt, provoked worse. I have destroyed all trace evidence or hoarded every shred of proof. I have taken a picture of a photograph after lighting it on fire in the desert. I have let meaningless flaws and differences of opinion ruin an otherwise sublime relation. I have assumed that I was doing the right thing or I have known for a fact that I was making a huge mistake. I have tried to believe that everything happens for a reason, though I deem this philosophy to be craven and malevolent. I have pined and I have languished, and I am convinced that I have been in love. I cannot speak for anyone else.

TRUCE

On Thanksgiving morning, I gulp down triplicate
diet pills so I don't have to eat.
Unafflicted with an invitation anywhere, the gym closed,
I sit on a bench facing Bristol Harbor.
This is Rhode Island and that's ocean water.
Maybe I should drive up to the State House
with the Quakers and act useful,
but I stick to this cracked white bench and think of women
in coffee shops writing in leather-bound journals,
cups of adult herbal tea at the ready,
their calm separateness foreboding as boiling oil.
I'm over-and-done-with, a set of monkey bones in outer space.
I can't even take pleasure
in the perpetuity of shimmering marina,
bright orange buoys, and the eccentricity of sailboats
still anchored out of season, naked masts too proud to move.
I look straight through the occasional jogger or cyclist
preemptively working off an engorgement.
Mute sea gulls plunge along the jagged shore,
gloating on the wing and hunting for scraps, ancillary to nothing.
I consider reading a book, and then here comes this old man.
There's no other way to put it.
Here. He. Comes.
The guy's in his sixties, at least, and he's wearing baggy,
dark blue pants and a light blue windbreaker,
his dirty flannel shirt untucked underneath.
What hair he has left is short and silver;
he keeps rubbing his tonsure like he can't believe it.
He walks carefully down the bike path,

angling toward the shallows, trying to find a particular spot.
He doesn't look drunk exactly.
Something in the air feels like suicide or honor
or an impossibly expensive promise.
I half-expect him to wade out into the surf
and swim for the shipping lanes, but he stops at the rocks.
As he reaches inside his pocket and takes out a necklace
the sun smears across the sky.
While he leans over and washes the necklace
the sea sparkles like chewed glass.
For a moment, as they say, my veins stop pumping their dark
       ars poetica.
I want to feel calm. I want to feel calm. Please, let me feel calm.

Confessions of a
L=A=N=G=U=A=G=E Poet

I'm afraid of needles. I get nauseous listening to news anchors talk about blood drives. I close my eyes during intravenous drug use scenes in the art films I rent from Blockbuster.

I'm a very meticulous person, though I find the word "person" oppressive.

I believe in a world that remains just out of earshot,
but don't tell anyone.

Making sense only makes sense when you're falling from a dirigible with no parachute—and that only happens in real life.

Sometimes I mistake genitals for an energy field. I'm addicted to scrambled porn.

I like my women barefoot and incomprehensible.
My men, too.

Sentences make me feel claustrophobic.

Surgically, I had my heart replaced with a gumball machine full of toenails.

I can prove that reaching out from beyond the grave is needy.

Calling all cars! Calling all cars! You know what I mean?

I hate poetry that tries to wet itself and can't.

William Carlos Williams was a baby-killer.
He put the litter in literature.

Tug boats on the East River act too cutesy-pooh.

I live in abject fear of making a point, of being understood.
Therefore: Death to all code-breakers!

Whenever I move into a new apartment, for the first few months,
every dark spot on the wall looks like a roach.

I have used the word "red" as a preposition.

My excuses have excuses, so when anyone says, "There's no
excuse," I respond, "There's always an excuse" and,
besides, having no excuse is itself a major excuse.

Once, my cousin hit me in the head with an infant.

When I dispose of my victims, the readers, I chop them
into a random number of chunks, and I mail the chunks
to addresses I pluck out of those old-fashioned
telephone books you find at the library,
the kind with the names in alphabetical order.
The zip codes I locate on the Internet.

I prefer Anti-NyQuil to NyQuil.

I destroy from within.

Until I have achieved total airport boredom in my writing,
I will never be satisfied.
Then why don't I take a vow of silence, you ask?

Exactly.

A Burden

They lounge around an above-ground swimming pool
behind a trailer in East Tennessee,
my mother, my sister, my mother's sister.
They range from plump to morbidly obese,
an emotionally exhausted tableau,
their various ailments accurate as mean time
in the heavy August heat.
Short-horned grasshoppers and cicadas
provide the incidental music
but there's no breeze to take the edge off, no radio.
These women have fashioned a living
out of multiple marriages, social security disability,
and the odd class action suit.
Not bad for people who started with nothing.

Durable as a canvas punching bag,
my mother survived breast cancer, colon cancer,
and today she has inoperable carcinoma of the lungs.
Her every statement, her every gesture,
upstages Prometheus bestowing fire.
Can she soak in the pool wearing her morphine patch?
How long can she stay in the sun
with skin the color and texture of mashed potatoes?
Her mood is vulnerable, confessional.
So near the end, she needs to clear her name.
She needs to convince her children
that they could have been raised worse.
Nobody fired us out of a cannon or turned us into stew.
The commissar never sold us off to NASCAR.

As the Q & A becomes more A than Q,
and disclaimers smuggle in a meddle of claims,
my mother says, "When I was a kid I caught
my brother Turner having sex with a chicken."
Cue the foreboding twisted rope sound
of a catapult cranked and loaded.
My sister bursts into tears.
My aunt wishes she could drown everyone in the pool.
My mother pleads dementia and picks at a scab.
Turner's an undiagnosed manic-depressive,
golf-playing, retired gym teacher now,
a low level charmer who hatched a dozen
get-rich-quick schemes that never panned out.
He's a respectable guy and doesn't deserve
the infamy a family exhumes when death
blows up the party balloons.

If he fucked a chicken, he fucked it in Kentucky,
where he and my mother came of age,
raised by dirt farmers in a shack with a dirt floor.
Out front, the mailbox had rusted shut.
Back by the creek slumped a windowless chicken coop.
Maybe Turner stood among the perches
and nesting boxes candling eggs,
a juvenile dungeoned in Appalachia.
One thing led to another.
Christ, all the girls in the valley were kin.
His innocent libidinousness forced him to make
a choice that philosophers and screenwriters dream about.
There's no cause for elaboration,
no cause for imagery or epithet—

because draining, plucking, and evisceration
required haste to keep the meat from spoiling on the bone.
Any truth to this story lasted less than five minutes.

As the women of my clan descend into rosy resentment,
a callus of secrecy hardens around the telling.
The sun melts across the surrounding hills,
another summer afternoon spent buried alive.
Soon, my mother will head north
for Ohio to be closer to her brother,
and the cancer will spread to her brain.
He visits her every day at the nursing home.
They have so many tests and pills in common.
Perhaps she had to degrade him with her memory
before she would let him sit quietly beside her,
hold her hand, sometimes finish her applesauce
or roll the portable toilet up to the bed.
And when she falls asleep he never forgets
to turn the TV off as he leaves.

BED, BATH, AND BEYOND

Days, maybe weeks, before the first
whole night together,
I ventured down Second Avenue
to buy a new pillowcase for the optional
third pillow, your pillow.
In the past, there had been
a maroon pillowcase
and a navy blue pillowcase
and a bottle-green pillowcase.
One refused to accept bribes;
one pretended to drink holy water;
one took a full-time job crying.

According to the packaging,
your pillowcase is oyster, obliterates
the selfishness of regret,
and looks like a fresh sheet of paper
against your brown skin,
your brown skin that seems
so crucial and complementary
against my white skin
in the warm, reflective dark.
Now that my body feels like a pulpit,
and I am my body's messenger,
I will keep this life.

2002

Among the Musk Ox People, Mary Ruefle
What it Wasn't, Laura Kasischke
The Finger Bone, Kevin Prufer
The Late World, Arthur Smith
Slow Risen Among the Smoke Trees, Elizabeth Kirschner
Keeping Time, Suzanne Cleary
Astronaut, Brian Henry

2003

Imitation of Life, Allison Joseph
A Place Made of Starlight, Peter Cooley
The Mastery Impulse, Ricardo Pau-Llosa
Except for One Obscene Brushstroke, Dzvinia Orlowsky
Taking Down the Angel, Jeff Friedman
Casino of the Sun, Jerry Williams
Trouble, Mary Baine Campbell
Lives of Water, John Hoppenthaler

2004

Freeways and Aqueducts, James Harms
Tristimania, Mary Ruefle
Prague Winter, Richard Katrovas
Venus Examines Her Breast, Maureen Seaton
Trains in Winter, Jay Meek
The Women Who Loved Elvis All Their Lives, Fleda Brown
The Chronic Liar Buys a Canary, Elizabeth Edwards
Various Orbits, Thom Ward

2005

Laws of My Nature, Margot Schilpp
Things I Can't Tell You, Michael Dennis Browne
Renovation, Jeffrey Thomson
Sleeping Woman, Herbert Scott
Blindsight, Carol Hamilton
Fallen from a Chariot, Kevin Prufer
Needlegrass, Dennis Sampson
Bent to the Earth, Blas Manuel De Luna

2006

Burn the Field, Amy Beeder
Dog Star Delicatessen: New and Selected Poems 1979–2006,
    Mekeel McBride
The Sadness of Others, Hayan Charara
A Grammar to Waking, Nancy Eimers
Shinemaster, Michael McFee
Eastern Mountain Time, Joyce Peseroff
Dragging the Lake, Robert Thomas

2007

So I Will Till the Ground, Gregory Djanikian
Trick Pear, Suzanne Cleary
Indeed I Was Pleased With the World, Mary Ruefle
The Situation, John Skoyles
One Season Behind, Sarah Rosenblatt
The Playhouse Near Dark, Elizabeth Holmes
Drift and Pulse, Kathleen Halme
Black Threads, Jeff Friedman
On the Vanishing of Large Creatures, Susan Hutton

2008

The Grace of Necessity, Samuel Green
After West, James Harms
The Book of Sleep, Eleanor Stanford
Anticipate the Coming Reservoir, John Hoppenthaler
Parable Hunter, Ricardo Pau-Llosa
Convertible Night, Flurry of Stones, Dzvinia Orlowsky

2009

Divine Margins, Peter Cooley
Cultural Studies, Kevin A. Gonzalez
Cave of the Yellow Volkswagen, Maureen Seaton
Group Portrait from Hell, David Schloss
Birdwatching in Wartime, Jeffery Thomson
Dear Apocalypse, K. A. Hays
Warhol-o-rama, Peter Oresick

2010

Admission, Jerry Williams
The Other Life: Selected Poems, Herbert Scott
In the Land We Imagined Ourselves, Jonathan Johnson
The Diminishing House, Nicky Beer
Selected Early Poems: 1958-1983, Greg Kuzma
Say Sand, Daniel Coudriet
A World Remembered, T. Alan Broughton
Knock Knock, Heather Hartley